# Mountains

by Alison Adams

## Table of Contents

What Is a Mountain?............................................... 2
How Are Mountains Formed? ..................................... 4
Where Are Mountains?............................................. 6
What Are the Different Parts of a Mountain?.......... 8
Glossary and Index ................................................ 20

# What Is a Mountain?

A **mountain** is a part of the land that is much higher than the land around it.

This is the highest mountain in the world.

This is **Mount Everest**.
It is in the **Himalayas**.
It is more than 25,000 feet high.

# How Are Mountains Formed?

Many mountains are made
when one part of the land
pushes against another part of the land.
The land pushes up and forms mountains
where the two parts meet.

Mountains can take many years to form.
Even after they have formed,
they continue to grow and change.

# How Some Mountains Are Formed

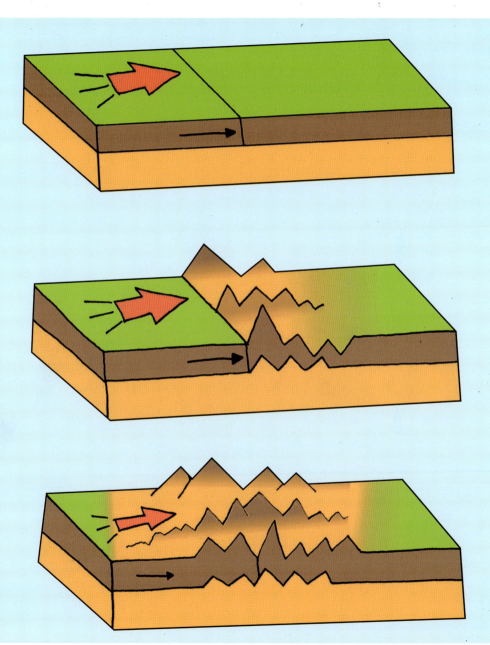

# Where Are Mountains?

There are mountains all over the world. Groups of mountains that formed together are called **mountain ranges**.

This is a mountain range in the Rocky Mountains.

This map shows you where some of the largest mountain ranges are.

## Mountain Ranges Around the World

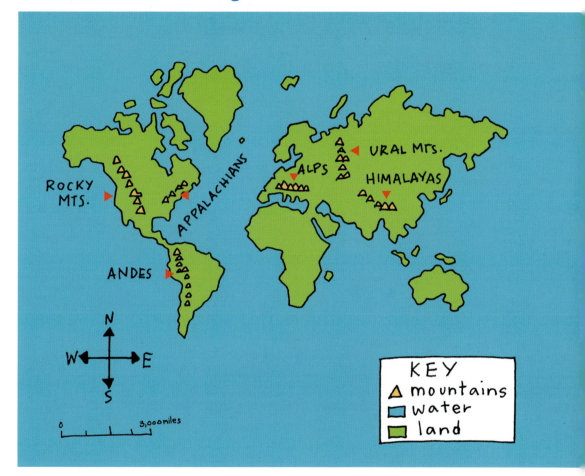

Can you find where the mountains on page 3 are located?

# What Are the Different Parts of a Mountain?

The warmest part of a mountain is at the bottom. The temperature gets colder higher up the mountain.
The coldest part is at the top.
It is often covered with snow.
Different kinds of plants and animals live on the different parts of a mountain.

# Levels of a Mountain

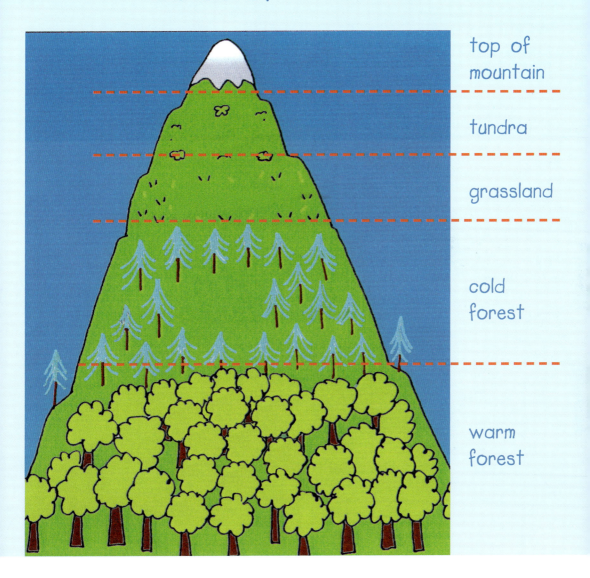

The height and location of a mountain determine how many parts, or levels, the mountain has.

This is the very bottom part of one mountain. **warm forest** grows here. The trees in this forest lose their leaves in the winter.

Trees that lose their leaves are called deciduous.

Many animals live in the warm forest. This animal hardly ever comes down from the trees. It gets water from dew and raindrops.

This animal is a **golden langur**.

This is the next part on the mountain. A **cold forest** grows here. The trees in this forest do not lose their leaves in the winter. They stay green all year long.

Trees that do not lose their leaves are called **evergreen trees**.

This animal lives in the cold forest.
It likes to climb the trees.
It must eat almost all day
to get enough food.

This animal is a **red panda**.

Another part of the mountain is too high for trees. It is too cold and windy for tall plants to grow. Only grass and small plants can grow on this part of the mountain.

This part, or level, is called a **grassland**.

Some animals live here, too.
This animal has strong legs to help it climb the tall hills.

This animal is a **takin**.

The next part of the mountain is covered with snow most of the year. It is so cold that only a few plants can grow.

This part, or level, of the mountain is called the **tundra**.

Here is an animal that lives on this part of the mountain. It has a thick coat of fur to keep it warm. It hunts other animals for food.

This is a **snow leopard**. For many years, people hunted this animal for its fur. There are not many snow leopards left in the world.

This is the **summit**, or top, of the mountain. Only snow and rock are here. It is so cold and windy here that nothing can grow.

Few animals live at the top of the mountain. But here is one animal you might see. Its strong wings help it fly near the top of the mountain.

Find out what mountain is closest to where you live. What plants and animals live there?

This bird is a **lammergeier**.

## Glossary

**cold forest** (KOLD FOR-est): a forest with evergreen trees

**evergreen trees** (EH-ver-green TREEZ): trees that stay green all year

**golden langur** (GOLE-den LAHN-ger): a thin, long-limbed monkey that lives in Asia

**grassland** (GRAS-land): an area with grass and small plants

**Himalayas** (hih-muh-LAY-uhz): a mountain range located in Asia

**lammergeier** (LA-mer-gy-er): a large bird that lives in the mountains of Europe and Asia

**Mount Everest** (MOWNT EH-vuh-rist): the highest mountain in the world, located in the Himalayas

**mountain** (MOWN-tun): an area of land that is much higher than the land around it

**mountain ranges** (MOWN-tun RANJE-ez): large groups of mountains

**red panda** (RED PAN-duh): a small animal with reddish fur that lives in Asia

**snow leopard** (SNOH LEH-perd): a large cat with long, thick fur that lives in the mountains of Asia

**summit** (SUH-mit): the top of a mountain

**takin** (TAH-keen): a large, shaggy animal that lives in the mountains of Asia

**tundra** (TUN-druh): a cold, often snowy area where only low plants can grow

**warm forest** (WORM FOR-est): a forest with trees that lose their leaves in winter

## Index

cold forest, 9, 12–13
evergreen trees, 12
golden langur, 11
grassland, 9, 14
Himalayas, 2, 7
lammergeier, 19
mountain ranges, 6–7

Mount Everest, 2
red panda, 13
snow leopard, 17
summit, 18
takin, 15
tundra, 16
warm forest, 9–11